— And the —
WORD
BECAME FLESH

A Book of Christian Poetry and Microfiction

Peace, Joy, and Love Encompass the Spirit of God

DORIS H. DANCY

And the
WORD
BECAME FLESH

A Book of Christian Poetry and Microfiction

He Bore the Cross for Us That We Might Be
Justified and Wear a Crown

"Blessed is the man who endures temptation; for when he has been approved, he will receive the crown of life which the Lord has promised to those who love Him."

James 1:12

DORIS H. DANCY

Lightning Fast Book Publishing, LLC
www.lfbookpublishing.com

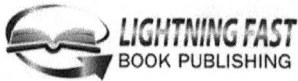

LIGHTNING FAST
BOOK PUBLISHING

ISBN: 978-1-7348113-8-4

Table of Contents

Dedication xi

Acknowledgements xiii

Foreword.. 1

Introduction.. 3

The Gift

And the Word Became Flesh 9

He Dwelt Among Us 11

His Word... 12

A Morning Prayer.. 13

Grace.. 14

The Gift of Forgiveness 15

Why Gaze into Heaven?.. 17

Our Reflections

Are We Branded with the Master's Touch?...................... 21

Cease To Struggle 22

What Do You Believe?... 24

The Decision 26

His Plan

Prayer for A Godly Mission...31

Just An Ordinary Day...32

His Majestic Call 34

His Love

A Precious Gift from God 39

In The Nick of Time..40

In His Eyes...42

Quality...44

Her Big Brown Eyes 45

Where Is Love?...47

There You Are 48

How Do You Say Good-Bye To Friends? 50

Relationships
(Microfiction Stories)

Golden Moments Remembered 55

God Waves Red Flags..56

Kill, Steal, and Destroy..57

A Sacrificial Heart 58

The Significance of Life's Decisions....................................59

Angels Watching 60

From Luke 24:15-16..61

About The Author...63

"I will bless the Lord at all times,
His praise shall continually be in my mouth.

My soul shall make its boast in the Lord,
The humble shall hear of it and be glad.

Oh, magnify the Lord with me,
And let us exalt His name together.

Psalm 34:1-3

In Honor of

Presiding Elder
Sidney Wesley Williams, Jr.

I will forever be grateful to the late Presiding Elder Sidney W. Williams, Jr who always inspired me with his words of wisdom. He consistently helped me understand that there is a need to look a little deeper every time you study the Word of God. He spent hours explaining, teaching, and giving me examples to illustrate the idea that when you think you have realized something profound about Jesus, look again because there is always more. He never failed to teach something special, which on my own, I know I never would have noticed, and now I know I never will forget.

Love,

Doris

In Honor of

Lieutenant General Donna W. Martin, 67th Inspector General of the United States Army

Lieutenant General Donna Martin, I am extremely proud of the awesome Godly woman you have become and mostly proud of the reciprocal gift you offer to Jesus Christ.

The Gift You Give

The gift presents first in your eyes. They're soft and welcoming. Your smile communicates an unmistakable friendliness. The ease in your manner conveys an approachable and welcoming nature that reminds me so much of your mom. In your very capable hands, Our Lord has placed an elevation He knows will not be misused and will not be foiled. The validation of your gift draws breath in a heart and soul filled with your humble spirit. It is your magnificent reciprocal gift of gratitude to Almighty God.

Dedication

To all of those in my youth who taught me and touched my life early with the Spirit of Christ:

**The Youth Adult Leaders at
St. Paul African Methodist Episcopal Church
Raleigh, North Carolina**

**The Nuns and Priests at
St. Monica's Catholic School
Raleigh, North Carolina**

To all of those who have continued to help me develop this close relationship with Christ as I grow to know Him more and more each day

A Special Dedication to:

Mom who taught me so much about His love through her words, her actions, and her wisdom.

Grandma who never let me forget that God is watching over me no matter what.

My constant friend, **Joyce A.R. Weeks,** who is always by my side without asking her to be. She is the one with that sixth sense that just calls and gives me whatever I need at the moment. She never lets me down. I am so blessed to have her in my life.

To my excellent friend, **Debra Hamilton Farley,** who never fails to tell me some special way to communicate the messages in my books. She is the one who stays in touch with what I need to do to make things better for my business, and she consistently gives me free and helpful advice. I will forever be grateful to her for her attention to me and her help in starting my successful business. She is a jewel.

My uncommon friend, **Rev. Barbara Dudley,** who listens to me in my weakest hours, strengthens me with our consistent study of the Word, and always prays with me through the sunshine and the rain in my life.

Acknowledgements

I thank God for the touch He has on my life. The strength of His presence is sometimes overwhelming. There are times when I think I'm writing, but He whispers that He's tapping out the words. I have experienced moments when I know His grace has saved me from some misstep, some car accident, some moment of anger, some slip of the tongue. It is this awareness that has brought me to this book of Christian poems and microfiction stories, all inspired by Him. I am grateful for my close relationship with Jesus Christ.

I thank my husband, Willie Dancy, Jr., for his constant love, support, and encouragement in every task I attempt. I can count on him to be always by my side.

I thank my daughters, Monica and Tara, for their support and help with thoughts, design, photography, editing, and encouragement. I am so grateful when I watch them dedicate so much of themselves to their love for Almighty God.

I am grateful to my in-laws who always support and encourage me. My sister-in-law, Elesta White, is one of my Beta readers, and I cannot thank her enough for her help.

Thank you to my Webmaster, Tracye McLean. She is a tremendous blessing to me. First of all, she is centered in Christ, and that alone opens the door to her creative spirit with all that

God puts in her hands to do. She is the keeper of my dream through the website, and it is consistently up to date, as well as informative in so many different areas. It is both beautiful and creative, and I am most grateful to this young lady for her example of who God wants us to be.

Thank you to my pastor, the Reverend Dr. Oretha P. Cross for the meaningful and thought-provoking sermons she preaches. They teach me, inspire me, and motivate me to study more. They help me build a closer relationship with God and learn more and more about the power that embodies the Spirit.

Thank you to each of my Beta readers, Jerome Chambers and Roxanna Reaves, for your critical eye and your honesty. My book is better because of you.

Thank you to my publisher, Matthew C. Horne of **Lightning Fast Book Publishing, LLC.** He is a unique publisher because he makes himself available to maximize an author's success. He has an eye for perfection, but most of all loves the Lord and is an excellent example to our youth as he continues to walk the path less traveled.

There are so many more that I could name from nieces, pastors, friends and acquaintances who have added something special to my knowledge of God. Sometimes, it has been as simple as a welcoming smile, a call to say "hi," a text, a card, and even a letter, especially from my friend John Scott (Scotty) who has made me bellow with laughter through the years. There are so many, and I am grateful for each of you.

Foreword

Doris H. Dancy's clear and irrefutable connection to her source—God—is evident in all of her literary offerings regardless of the genre. It's always a pleasure to read and publish her spiritual books because you walk away with a heightened and refined understanding of yourself through the revelation of God and His all-encompassing facets that reside in us all. *The Word Became Flesh* offers us all an opportunity to see God in various places and with a vastness we may have never ordinarily considered. The divinity of this work is obvious: when you learn to see God, you subsequently understand the blueprints to your own unique destiny. Doris H. Dancy is a consecrated vessel from which God freely pours His wisdom on humanity as a pure reflection of His love for us, His creation. I am not inspired to instruct you, the reader, to open yourself up to receive the anointed words in each poem. The pureness of the source of all creation—God—is having a conversation with Himself in you in every word of this divinely inspired book of poetry. I'm only inspired to encourage you to pay attention to what your Creator is revealing to you about yourself as you read this masterfully compiled collection of sacred poetry. Be still. Be peaceful. Be elevated in your knowledge of Your Creator; be elevated in the understanding of yourself to the finest degree. You have actual work and deposits to deliver to this world. Your mission and blueprint are only apparent when the voice of your Creator reigns supreme above all other voices, societal norms, opinions, and expectations in your life. Tune into every word on each page, and be the unique offering God intended for you to be to this world.

Matthew C. Horne,
Author/Motivational Speaker/Book Publisher

Introduction

Sometimes, I go outside in my backyard just to pray because there is something extra special about being surrounded by and enclosed in the beauty of nature. It gives the feel of the Savior's arms wrapped around me in His protective care. When I look up at the trees and a blue sky peeking through, I see Him. The sunlit spots that dance their way through the trees and settle on the forest floor is His way of revealing the quietness of His presence. When I find my way to the beach that is not very far from my home, it is amazing to hear the powerful roar of the ocean or the peaceful lapping of water as it washes up to shore. His presence is everywhere.

He says "Call to Me and I will answer you and show you great and mighty things that you do not know."(**Jeremiah 33:3**) Our Lord encourages us to form a close relationship with Him, promises that He will answer our call, and then gives us a magnificent bonus: He declares that He will open up some of His secrets to us. Wow! What a mighty God we serve.

Despite our occasional casual nod to Him and our daily distractions, He is always with us, always willing to hold out His hand to keep us from falling and always providing that "peace beyond understanding." He is a most amazing and incredible God who, in all of His splendor, consistently reaches out to us with mercy and with grace.

"And the Word Became Flesh," a short collection of poems and microfiction selections, will provide each of us another opportunity to spend some valuable quality time with Him. It will allow time to reflect on our own personal commitment to serve Him and to walk humbly in His presence. We will be reminded that He is the One who carries us when we are unable to carry ourselves. He is the One who provides comfort when life becomes unbearable and when we find it difficult to cope with the strangling forces surrounding us.

It is my hope and prayer that each of us will make a renewed commitment to Immanuel, *God With Us*, knowing if we simply surrender to Him, this is what we will know for sure and be able to say with certainty: "He is my Shepherd and I have everything I need. He lets me rest in green meadows; He leads me beside peaceful streams. He renews my strength. He guides me along the right paths, bringing honor to his name. Even when I walk through the dark valley of death, I will not be afraid, for You are close beside me. Your rod and Your staff protect and comfort me. You prepare a feast for me in the presence of my enemies. You welcome me as a guest, anointing my head with oil. My cup overflows with blessings. Surely Your goodness and unfailing love will pursue me all the days of my life, and I will live in the house of the Lord forever." **(Psalm 23 NIV)**

– Doris

"One thing I have desired of the Lord, that will I seek: that I may dwell in the house of the Lord all the days of my life, to behold the beauty of the Lord, and to inquire in His temple."

Psalm 27:4

In the beginning was the Word, and the Word was with God,
and the Word was God.

John 1:1

"*And the Word became flesh and dwelt among us,*
and we beheld His glory, the glory as of the only begotten
of the Father, full of grace and truth.

John 1:14

The Gift

AND THE WORD BECAME FLESH

"...And the Word became flesh and dwelt among us." (John 1:14)

"**W**hy?" you question...

To those who believe, here lies the Divine answer:

HE CAME

To do the will of God (John 6:38)

To bring good news of great joy (Luke 2:10)

To become a merciful and faithful high priest in the service of God (Hebrews 2: 17)

To humble Himself and become obedient to the point of death (Philippians 2:8)

To bear witness to the truth (John 18: 37)

HE CAME

To speak on God's authority (John 17:8)

To preach the Gospel (Luke 4:18-19)

To fulfil the Law and the Prophets (Matthews 5:17)

To put away sin by the sacrifice of Himself (Hebrews 9:26)

To be manifested that He might destroy the works of the devil (I John 3:8)

HE CAME

To seek and save that which was lost (Luke 19:10)

To be our peace (Ephesians 2:14)

To give Eternal life (John 6:51)

To be our Comforter (Isaiah 61: 1-3)

To send forth the Spirit of God's Son (Galatians 4:6)

HE CAME

To call sinners to repentance (Mark 2:17)

To shed light and defy darkness (John 12:46)

To come in the Name of the Father (John 5:43)

To serve and give His life a ransom for many (Mark 10:45)

To be glorified (John 12:23)

HE CAME

To die that we might be justified (John 12:24-27)

To sanctify Himself so we may be sanctified by truth

To reveal the Glory of God (John 1:14)

"And the Word became flesh and dwelt among us. . ."

"I have come as a light into the world that whoever believes in Me should not abide in darkness." John 12:46

He Dwelt Among Us:

To Save

To Preach

To Teach

To Heal

To Raise

To Create

To Provide

To Endure

To Pray

To Answer

To Guide

To Impart and

To love unconditionally.

"For the Son of Man has come to seek and to save that which was lost." Luke 19:10

His Word

His Word comes so gently,
Like the softness of snowflakes,
drifting silently to earth.
It settles peacefully on open hearts,
Then patiently waits to pour out a matchless love.
It guides our thoughts,
Covers our fears,
Ignites our hopes,
Anchors our dreams,
Calms our doubts,
Quiets our sorrows,
Shares our joys
And magnifies our gifts.
His Word comes so gently,
Like the soft breeze that quiets the heat of
summer's day.

"Your Word is a lamp to my feet and a light to my path."
Psalm 119:105

I woke early this morning, looked outside at the breaking of dawn, saw the magnificent beauty of God's offerings in this day, and whispered

A Morning Prayer

Lord, thank you for the sunlight filtering
through ancient trees,

For the earth that stands firm and
unshaken beneath my feet,

For the vastness and arc of a blue-sky hovering
above me in its majestic beauty,

For the breath in my lungs that gives me life today.

For I am as an ant in my world, tiny and vulnerable
to the Greatness in Yours, Infinite and Infallible.

So, draw a hedge of protection around us this day
as I ask for safety in Your arms.

"The effective fervent prayer of a righteous man avails much."
James 5:16

GRACE:

Sufficient, Unmerited, and Amazing

Grace is God's unmerited favor in the midst of our foolish
worldly ways of ingratitude and unforgiveness.
It is the sustainer, the constant helper that
answers when we call to Him.
Grace is the warmth of our Lord's abiding love.
It is His blessed assurance against the
coldness of life's fears.
It is His sustaining energizing strength in the
battle of earthly stress and turmoil.
It is the gift of circumstances untangled
in the labyrinth of confusion.
It is the power of His mighty conquering hand
in the clash of warring spirits.
Grace is the lift He provides when we
cannot walk alone.
It is the respite when we come boldly to His throne, seeking
help in times of trouble.
It is His fullness, His overflow that carries us
in our weakness.
Grace is the presence of the Holy Spirit
emboldened in us.
Grace is the living Christ, the Word made flesh,
who came and dwelled among us.

*"My grace is sufficient for you, for my strength is made perfect in
weakness." 2 Corinthians 12:9*

THE GIFT Of FORGIVENESS

The box is huge and shapeless and all locked in
It holds tightly to my weak tormented spirit.
  Harsh words destroying me,
  Unrequited love grieving me,
  Broken promises disappointing me,
  Futile lies condemning me,
  Cruel days battering me,
  Tear-filled nights sorrowing me,
  Sinister deeds depressing me.
Each is a piercing dagger to my soul.

I unwrap this box so carefully, fearfully, with dread.
  I take away red bows of sacrifice that sit atop my hate.
  I loose the tape that holds fast to the wretchedness inside of me.
  I pull away the paper that marks the devastation of my life .
Slowly...cautiously
  I lift the lid that hides an abyss of sorrow.

  Now, I clearly see the evil shadows that bend me to their will.

Surrendering in my despair, God alone fights the battle.
With His power and His might,
  I cast away the broken pieces,
  Smash to smithereens desired revenge,

Fling away the poisonous hate, and
Break the twisted vines of fury that entangled me.

When it is done, looking only to the Rock of my Salvation,
I ascend from the darkness and unfold in the Beauty of His Light.
He Bends to me and lifts me from my knees.
In His gentle, quiet voice, clearly, I hear His promise:
"I will be a ring of fire around her, and I will be the glory in her midst."

Finally, I am free from my Desert place.
In my hands, I hold a shimmering gift of love.
The FORGIVENESS that has been so difficult for me, now pervades my heart, and I soar with unbelievable joy, to the Glory Place.

"So My heavenly Father also will do to you, if each of you, from his heart, does not forgive his brother of his trespasses."
Matthew 18: 35

Why Gaze into Heaven?

Inspired by Mr. and Mrs. Frank Hendrick's
Sunday School Lesson

Why gaze into heaven?
The question is a captivating one
    asked so many years ago.
The answer, my friend, is the same today
    as ancient times before.
We gaze to know the Holy Spirit
    who dwells within us all.
We gaze with an expectation of
    a daily walk with Him.
We gaze to stay transfixed
    on the touch of His mighty right Hand.
We gaze to see Him revealed
    in the Spirit of Holiness.
We gaze to give thanksgiving
    for the purchase of our Salvation.
We gaze looking forward
    to His blessed coming again.

    So, why gaze into heaven?

Our gaze is an affirmation of our attentiveness to Him,
    a proof of an unyielding belief in His Return.

Jesus Christ, we gaze because You ascended there,
    sitting at the Right Hand of the Father, and

WE BELIEVE.

HALLELUJAH!

"...Ye men of Galilee, why stand ye gazing up into heaven?"
Acts 1:11

Reflections

Are We Branded with the Master's Touch?

*A*re we branded with the Master's Touch?
Does it show in the softness of loving eyes
That quietly, consistently seek out the Omniscient One?
Is our brand obvious in caring thoughts
that are filled with compassion?

Does our speech exemplify a spirit of humbleness?
Do our actions require no debt to pay?
Is there honesty and patience in our support?
Is trust evident in the smiles we wear?

Do our words express heartfelt blessings one to another?
Are our hands open to give?
Are our hearts willing to love?

Are we truly branded with the Master's Touch?
Is there evidence of some blessed assurance that
We have surrendered our hearts completely to Him?

How important it is to know for sure.

*"For God so loved the world that He gave His only begotten Son
that whoever believes in Him should not perish but have
everlasting life." John 3:16*

Cease To Struggle

A poem Inspired by Janet Boddie

If you think you can fix it, you can't.
If you think you know how, you don't.
If you think you can win all on your own,
Let me tell you for sure, you won't.
Yes, the struggles are real.
The hardships are true,
But only God can see you through.
He is the refuge.
He is the strength.
He is the present help.

He says in His Word to be still.
He declares that He is God.
So, cease to struggle.
Let His hand take control.

Yield to His will in the prayers that you pray,
For He promises peace
Far beyond what you say.
Rest in Him
Rely on His Word.
For sure, my friend,
This is what I know:

Lock away your desires,
And whatever you think,
Then cease to struggle.
Be still and wait.

"Trust in the Lord with all your heart, and lean not on your own understanding; In all your ways acknowledge Him and He will direct your paths." Proverbs 3:5-6

What Do You Believe?

Oh, children of the earth, what do you truly believe of God?
In your daily walk, do you notice Him?

Do you see Him in the flowers that bow in adoration to the
sun,
Or do you walk pass without a thought of His creative hand?

Do you hear Him whisper a blessing that helps you
        take each breath,
Or do you fail to thank Him for the air that gives you life?

Do you feel His touch of surrounding angels
        that keep you safe from harm,
Or do you think it is just coincidental that you see another day?

Do you smell the sweet aroma of His presence when you wake,
Or do you pass each precious moment distracted by the world?

Do you acknowledge His omnipotence for the gifts
        entrusted to your hand,
Or do you fail to yield the glory to the One who
        planned them all?

Do you seek His presence in the life He sacrificed for you,
Or do you consistently overlook the value
        in the Cross at Calvary?

Do you take some undistracted moments to study
      His precious Word,
Or do you give each second of every priceless day
      to some more menial task?

Do you acknowledge Him as Alpha, Omega,
      Beginning, and End,
Or do you mindlessly insult the inexorable grace
      and love He gives unconditionally to us all?

What, oh children of the earth, do you truly believe of God?

"But without faith it is impossible to please Him, for he who comes to God must believe that He is, and that He is a rewarder of those who diligently seek Him. Hebrews 11:6

The Decision

John 11:54, Jesus makes a decision:
To no longer move publicly among the people of Judea.
Instead, to withdraw to a village called Ephraim,
There to stay with His disciples.

You see, the people wanted to kill Him,
destroy Him,
keep Him inactive.
As a result, while He promised never to leave us or forsake us,
He vowed He would not remain public.

Oh, how shameful of them to be unfaithful to our Lord!
So, what of us today? Are we the same?

Do our actions keep Him private?
Do our voices silence Him,
Diminish, Rebuke Him,
And force Him into His private place refusing visibility?

In our waywardness, do we push Him into some private place?
Do we:
Hide Him?
Avoid Him?
Scorn His favor?

Deny His miracles?
Trample on His mercy and grace?
Make a mockery of His holiness?

Or do our actions:
Invite Him?
Include Him?
Honor and adore Him?

Do we engage Him,
Walk in His path,
Obey His voice,
Love and surrender to His Will?

Private or public Jesus,
The choice is ours alone.

> *"Therefore, Jesus no longer moved about publicly among the people of Judea. Instead, he withdrew to a region near the wilderness, to a village called Ephraim, where he stayed with his disciples."*
> *John 11:54*

His Plan

Prayer for A Godly Mission

Lord, we desire to follow the path you have designed for us.

Open our eyes to view a road less traveled,
and use this sight for Your Glory.

Prompt us to take the hand of others, those hands
You hand to us, and lead the way through the integral passage
where You wait in the Splendor of Your Glory.

Carry us over the Mountains,
Guide us through the Valleys,
Lift us across rough plains and crooked places.

Lead us gently to Your realm of unconditional love
where Understanding of Your ways awaits.

Touch our minds with Your powerful Insight
that we might serve You more.

"'For I know the plans I have for you,' declares the Lord, 'plans to prosper you and not to harm you, plans to give you a hope and a future.'" — Jeremiah 29:11.

Just an Ordinary Day

When Jesus calls us to Mission,
The stars won't fall,
The moon won't turn red,
The earth won't shake,
The lightning won't flash,
And the thunder won't roll.
It will be just an ordinary day.

It was just an ordinary day
When Moses left his home to tend Jethro's sheep,
BUT it was that day Jesus called him to be a prophet.

It was just an ordinary day
When David was called from shepherding his flock,
BUT it was that day Jesus anointed him King.

It was just an ordinary day
When Peter, Andrew, James, and John failed at netting fish,
BUT it was that day Jesus made them Fishers of Men.

It was just an ordinary day,
When Esther proclaimed, "If I perish, I perish."
BUT on that day, Jesus brought forth the Deliverer of the Jews.

So, if you are waiting for

The stars to fall,

The moon to turn red,

The earth to shake,

Lightning to flash,

Or thunder to roll,

Before you hear your call to Mission, wait no more.

It will be just an ordinary day.

So,

Answer His still, small voice, now.

Listen to His direction, now.

Pray for His guidance, now.

Oh, children of the earth,

"Sing unto the Lord a New Song

For He has done marvelous things.

Make a joyful noise unto the Lord all ye Earth,

And sing His praises" on just an ordinary day.

Declare his glory among the nations,
his marvelous deeds among all peoples.
I Chronicles 16:24

His Majestic Call

$\mathcal{H}$e calls in stillness, in a quietness that only He can manifest.
He whispers His sweet command of a plan
in the silence of a dream,

Or

In the midst of a single special moment,

Or

In the revelation of what might seem like an ordinary idea.

In our hands, He places this uncommon jewel of purpose.

With our acceptance,
Our faith,
Our decision to surrender to His will,
He molds the vision,
Sharpens the plan,
Creates the opportunity,
Pilots the direction,
AND
Opens the door to His Promises.

The dichotomy of bright stars and treacherous storms clash
and hollow out a rugged pathway,
Until in a magnificent burst of His Unimaginable Favor,
There emerges with Divine Truth

Some incredible moment,

Some unbelievable mastery

That actualizes, in our hands, the awesomeness
and faithfulness of

Almighty God.

And we know that all things work together for good to those who love God, to those who are the called according to His purpose.
Romans 8:28

His Love

A Precious Gift from God

Where do I begin to tell of a precious gift from God?
Do I begin when first the gift was given?

Somewhere in those deep and distant skies,
God created a masterpiece in you
To give us each a chance to view His eternal Love.

In your heart, He placed that golden light of affection,
And it casts a million rays of sun.
In your mind, He formed a will to give,
And a multitude reaps the benefits of your touch.
Your soul exudes that gentle, quiet spirit
That easily keeps touch with humankind.

There is no need to tell of precious gifts from God.
He gave us eyes to see your beauty
and a heart to know your love.

*". . . we do not lose heart. Even though our outward man is
perishing, yet the inward man is being renewed day by day."*
2 Corinthians 4:16

In the Nick of Time

Written for Rev. Dr. Oretha P. Cross
In Appreciation for the Beauty of Your Spirit

God sent you to us
 In the nick of time.

Because of Pastor Donald White's death,
Our hearts were heavy when you came.
We had cried, mourned, and given way to that stone-like feeling
that inevitably comes with the realization of loss.

We were trying desperately to get used to another voice,
another way, another time,
And then you came.

You came with a radiant smile that warmed us.
You came with a spirit that lifted us,

But most of all, you came with a powerful Word
that reminded us that He never leaves, never forsakes,
and always has a plan to move us closer to Him.

Thank you.

Thank you for your love, your care, and your vision
that presently finds us in a soft and restful place.

*"The eyes of the Lord are toward the righteous and his ears
toward their cry." Psalm 34:15*

In His Eyes

Inspired by my Granddaughter, Tali Dancy

In middle school, they laugh,
    They tease,
        And relentlessly taunt.
            They pick, pick, pick!

They say I'm too tall,
    Too skinny,
        Too fat,
            Too short.

They shout their evil words:
    " Your lips are too thick,
        Too thin.
            Your hair too kinky,
                Too long,
                    Too straight."

They try so hard to crush my spirit with hate-filled words, to stomp my heart 'til shattered pieces fall,' til teardrops melt my soul away and drown me in Insecurity.

But I will not yield!
    I will not bow or bend to them
Because I know a powerful secret:

I am beautifully and wonderfully made by nail-pierced Hands-
those Hands created us all -

All different,
     All special,
          All perfect
In His Eyes.

"For the Lord does not see as man sees; for man looks at the
outward appearance, but the Lord looks at the heart."
I Samuel 16:7

Quality

The quality of what you do is indicative of you.
It speaks your name and tells exactly who you are.
It is the height to which you allow your mind to climb.
It is what some have called "the ceiling of dreams."
It is the depth of your struggle,
The width of your gain,
The consistency of all you wish to be.

It is your self-worth conceptualized
and magnified a trillion times.
It is the strength of your grasp on the soul of potentiality.
It is the level of your understanding,
The degree of your goals,
The sum total of all you decide to be.
The quality of what you do is indicative of you.
It speaks your name and tells exactly who you are.

*Do your best to present yourself to God as one approved, a worker
who has no need to be ashamed, rightly handling the word of
truth. 2 Timothy 2:15*

Her Big Brown Eyes

Dedicated to My Mom, Mrs. Mildred Birdsall Hodge

"*Mares eat oats and does eat oats
and little lambs eat ivy*"

That was our first song
And we would laugh,
And she would tickle me,
And we would roll on the floor,
Always with her big brown eyes
Looking down on me.

Somewhere between then and my teen years
There were boys in my life,
And parties with keepsakes,
And movies that brought both laughter and tears,
But always there was that strong partnership,
And big brown eyes that kept me safe.

College came and went, and I left home,
And a fellow entered my life.
There was a wedding
With special dinners,
Congratulations and well wishes,
And even then, in all of my excitement of
A new and promising life,
Nothing meant more to me than the

Big brown eyes smiling at me
with pride and unconditional love.

There was this teaching job,
A lovely new home,
Then two beautiful daughters that would look to him
        and me for love and protection.
There were visits to Raleigh with
Hugs and kisses and that feeling of familiar safety.
Days later, our visit would end,
And in our car, ready to leave,
I'd look back and see the big brown eyes still whispering,
"Be careful. Take care. I love you."

Months melted into years,
And time took its toll.
The hair turned gray, and the body grew weak,
But her smiling eyes stayed the same.
On our last days together,
When memories were only mine,
I sat with her and held her hand.
When the clock ticked time to go,
I said goodbye, and she said not a word,
But lifted her hand and let it say so long,
And the big brown eyes kissed me a final time
With their everlasting and unconditional love.

*Honor your father and your mother, that your days may be long in
    the land that the LORD your God is giving you. Exodus 20:12*

Where is Love?

You'll find Love in the majesty of a sunrise,
And in the beauty of its nightly bow to Him.
It's in the sparkle of a morning's crystal dewdrop,
And in the hues that rest on wings of butterflies.
You'll find Love in the sway of soft green grasses,
And in the gentle breeze of playful summer's day.
It's in the sweet caress that bathes the night in silence,
And in the power of a twinkling starlit sky.
You'll find Love in the velvet cloak that drapes a quiet sea,
And in God's hidden treasures on an ancient ocean floor.
It's in the beauty of an icy snow-capped mountaintop,
And in the fog that swallows up the giant forest trees.
You'll find Love in the bouncing dance of busy humming bees,
And in the yielding of earth's fragrance from the rose.
It's in the energetic rhythms of nature's symphonic band,
And in the heart that knows the Maker of it all.

And one called out to another and said, "Holy, Holy, Holy, is the Lord of hosts, The whole earth is full of His glory." Isaiah 6:3

There You Are

Inspired by Presiding Elder Sidney W. Williams Jr.

There you are. I see You. You're in the morning mist,
Glistening like diamond sparkles in the shimmering sunlight
of the day.

There you are. I see you in a yellow moon
Hanging lazily in a
Darkened sky.

There you are again. You can't hide from me.
You make me smile. I see you in the redness, the pinkness,
and the yellowness of roses whose perfumed scent rides
on the shoulders of soft breezes.

There You are. I hear You. You're whispering in tall pines and
majestic oaks gently swaying in the solitude of forest green.

You are in crashing waves that leap to touch the sky.
I see You in grains of sand on distant shores.

There You are in fluffy white clouds riding against the backdrop
of vast blueness. You show Yourself in silvery raindrops
that soak the earth, and in weeping willows refusing
to cry a single tear.

There You are. I see You. You only hide from those who refuse
to see. Regardless, You are always there, always present.
The One who cares to remind us if we only look, if we dare
to take a chance on FAITH.

You will never leave, never forsake me. You PROMISED.
The message is clear if we simply BELIEVE: *"Here, I AM."*

There You are, the essence of unimaginable LOVE.
I see You fluttering daily on the wings of a soft invisible breeze
and in the bright twinkling star that long ago brightened
an ancient manger bed.

"Know therefore today, and take it to your heart, that the Lord, He
is God in heaven above and on the earth below; there is no other."
Deuteronomy 4:39

How Do You Say Goodbye to Friends?

How Do You Say Goodbye to Friends?
Do you casually say so long and somewhere deep inside,
whisper, "yes, so long . . ."
So long as this old heart beats firmly in my breast,
I'll have a panoramic view of you and me doing so many things,
thinking so many thoughts, feeling, and I'll not forget."

So, how do you say goodbye to friends?

Do you meet with tear-stained eyes,
and slowly lift your hand,
and let it say goodbye?
Maybe you reach behind the eyes
And read the secret messages they hold:
We'll never part, for single special moments
have the capacity to ride upon the wind,
where they can meet in time and space
through mind and soul.

So, how do you say goodbye to friends?

Do you bid a formal farewell? Adieu?
Do you add a foreign touch and say
Adios, auf Wiedersehen, sayonara, au revoir?

Maybe you giggle just a little
to hold on, for a second,
to the closeness you have shared.
How do you say goodbye?

I choose not to say goodbye at all,
but rather to express simply this:
Thank you for letting me touch your life
and share a part of you
that I will forever hold
in the shadows of my mind.
I love you and God bless.

*"A man who has friends must himself be friendly, but there is a
friend that sticks closer than a brother." Proverbs 18:24*

Microfiction

Microfiction is a genre where the author is challenged to write a story in no more than one hundred words. The title of the work is not counted. I am fascinated with this form and decided to try my hand at it and include some of my new one hundred-word stories here.

When we think of God and all that He has created, it is amazing to realize the millions of stories that live with us daily. All of the stories included here are fiction except for one personal miracle. I hope you enjoy reading these short realistic experiences that touch our lives in so many different ways.

Relationships

Golden Moments Remembered

It was missing for three years, and for three years, she had been missing him. That unforgettable golden locket hid itself behind the old chest. Its sight had escaped the vacuum and dust mop. Today the sun caught a glimpse of it, and the sparkle revealed its hiding place. Her aging eyes had seen it a million times in the shadows of her mind, and in this mesmerizing moment, it danced again around her youthful neck. Her wrinkled fingers stretched across the years and touched again the starlit night when he introduced the locket to her with a lasting kiss.

"He who finds a wife finds what is good and receives favor from the LORD." Proverbs 18:22

God Waves Red Flags

Shannon checked messages again. The last cube melted in Brandon's tea. Earlier, he'd zipped her silver gown; she'd straightened his tie, and they kissed.

"Meet you in a few, Shan. Gotta run. It's important."

"This prestigious award is important! Where is he?" she muttered.

"They called your name, Sis. Go!"

Meanwhile, in darkness, he sat secretly at Britney's wedding.

"You're so selfish!" she'd shouted at him a year ago.

Those words still angered him as he stood up to skulk out with old resentments and jealousies intact.

"Nope! Don't need either of them!"

"You should know this, Timothy, that in the last days there will be very difficult times. For people will love only themselves and their money. They will be boastful and proud, scoffing at God, disobedient to their parents, and ungrateful. They will consider nothing sacred. They will be unloving and unforgiving; they will slander others and have no self-control. They will be cruel and hate what is good." II Timothy 3:1-3

Kill, Steal, and Destroy

It's extremely difficult to look at the open wound. The hurt is enormously deep. Her words ring in my young ears, and my heart surrenders to unbelievable defeat, disappointment, insecurity, depression, and feelings that I cannot even identify.

"You're just like your daddy-no good. You'll never be anything but nothing!"

What did I do to deserve her looks of hate, her words of pain? Maybe I will never know because the open wound is too painful to touch. Sticks and stones may break bones, but, without God, words can **kill** the spirit, **steal** the heart, **and destroy** a beautiful life.

The thief comes only to steal and kill and destroy. I came that they may have life and have it abundantly. John 10:10

A Sacrificial Heart

He left in my seventeenth year, the night I told him the baby was his. Nine months later, Skyla was born. Twenty-one years later, I sit in this company of graduates finding her name listed as magna cum laude. I secretly smile, remembering first piano recitals, trips to dance studios and competitions, honor society inductions, the struggles to get that "A," and a screeching violin that never worked for her. I look down at my scarred hands from too many jobs and years of love and determination. Quietly, I thank God she has taken the road less traveled.

"Love is patient, love is kind. It does not envy, it does not boast, it is not proud. ⁵ It does not dishonor others, it is not self-seeking, it is not easily angered, it keeps no record of wrongs. ⁶ Love does not delight in evil but rejoices with the truth. ⁷ It always protects, always trusts, always hopes, always perseveres."
I Corinthians 13:4-7

The Significance of Life's Decisions

The sound of the ocean made me happy. There was something mesmerizing and freeing about its crashing waves or water lapping at the shore. I sat on the rocks looking out at the morning sun glistening on the ocean's blue coat and whispered a prayer. I could finally pray again, and I was thankful. I was no longer angry with Him and could now admit it was my fault. I chose to drive in a downpour and stop at a bar. It was my fault I wrecked my shiny new SUV and the life of someone I had never met.

"He leads me beside the still waters.
He restores my soul . . ." Psalm 23: 2b

Angels Watching

(Personal true story)

It was a sunny day, one of those days perfect for shopping, and I was free to do just that. The drive was down Mercury Boulevard, and I was happily singing a hymn with Kirk Franklin on the radio. Then it happened. The 18-wheeler in front of me slammed on his brakes; I slammed on mine. I yanked the steering wheel to avoid running into him. All of a sudden, my car flew backward. What? I glanced behind me, and no one was there except my guardian angel.

"For He will command His angels concerning you to guard you in all your ways. On their hands they will bear you up, lest you strike your foot against a stone." -Psalm 91:11-12

From Luke 24:15-16

Finally! A car, a slammed door, a rattling key in the lock. Macy whispered a "thank you" to God. It was her teen daughter coming in after 2 AM.

"Where have you been?"

The question ignited drunken foul words and senseless accusations.

"You're just nosey, out of touch with the REAL world."

Alone in her room, this mother prayed a fervent prayer.

Morning brought a soft knock at her door and a loving embrace.

"Mom, I'm sorry," she whispered.

Instantly, unlike the men walking to Emmaus, **Macy knew Him** and felt His presence.

"So it was, while they conversed and reasoned,
that Jesus Himself drew near and went with them.
But their eyes were restrained, so that they did not know Him."
-Luke 24:15-16

Be Still and Know
that I Am God.

-Psalm 46:10

About The Author

Doris H. Dancy is an accomplished and award-winning educator, writer, speaker, playwright, novelist, a church officer, and a member of the Lambda Omega Chapter of Alpha Kappa Alpha Sorority, Inc. She received her BA Degree in English and Spanish Education at North Carolina Central University in Durham, North Carolina, and her MA Degree in English Education from Hampton University in Hampton, Virginia. Dancy has been a Teacher of English, High School English Department Chairperson, English Teacher Specialist, and Supervisor of English K-12 for Hampton City Public Schools. She is the author of the Redemptive Love Series: *Jagged Edges*, *Shattered Pieces* and *All Other Ground*. Each novel has received numerous awards.

Mrs. Dancy is married to Willie Dancy, Jr. and they have two daughters, Monica Dancy-Hayes and Tara Dancy Abaya. They have three beautiful granddaughters: Cadence, Tali, and Zoey.

To learn more about Doris H. Dancy, please visit: www.dorishdancy.com

Additional Titles
By Author, Doris H. Dancy

The Redemptive Love Series

All Other Ground

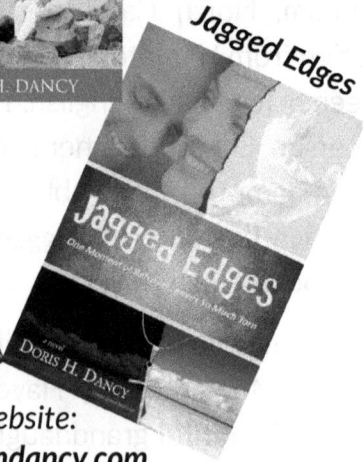

Shattered Pieces

Jagged Edges

My website:
www.dorishdancy.com

Awards

1. Readers' Favorite Five Star Award
2. USA Best Book Awards Finalist
3. International Book Award Finalist
4. 3-in-1 The Voice Book Award for Christian Writers

Available At: www.dorishdancy.com

www.ingramcontent.com/pod-product-compliance
Lightning Source LLC
Chambersburg PA
CBHW071110090426
42737CB00013B/2558